R☩YAL
WISDOM

THE MOST DAFT, CHEEKY, AND BRILLIANT QUOTES FROM BRITAIN'S ROYAL FAMILY

KATE PETRELLA

Adamsmedia
AVON, MASSACHUSETTS

Published by
Adams Media, a division of F+W Media, Inc.
57 Littlefield Street, Avon, MA 02322. U.S.A.
www.adamsmedia.com

ISBN 10: 1-4405-2745-8
ISBN 13: 978-1-4405-2745-6
eISBN 10: 1-4405-2756-3
eISBN 13: 978-1-4405-2756-2

Printed in the United States of America.

10   9   8   7   6   5   4   3   2   1

Library of Congress Cataloging-in-Publication Data
is available from the publisher.

Many of the designations used by manufacturers and sellers to distinguish their product
are claimed as trademarks. Where those designations appear in this book and Adams
Media was aware of a trademark claim, the designations have been printed with initial
capital letters.

Illustration credits:
Prince of Wales crown © istock.com / David Bukach; crown borders, scrolling shield, and
crown crest © istock.com / Cloudniners; London buildings, car, and bus © istock.com /
Lenotura; Phone box © istock.com / John_ Woodcock.

This book is available at quantity discounts for bulk purchases.
For information, please call 1-800-289-0963.

CONTENTS

INTRODUCTION

"My sense of humor will get me into trouble one day."

Prince Charles was right—except that it's gotten him into trouble on more than one occasion. And he's not alone. Prince Philip admits that he's gaffe prone, and Camilla, Duchess of Cornwall, has sometimes found herself saying things that don't come out quite the way she intended.

Whether the royals' humor is intentionally funny or misconstrued, biting or bantering, dry or daft, it reminds us that although these people were born into extraordinary circumstances, they are, after all, ordinary human beings, just like the rest of us. The trappings of their lives are vastly different from ours, but humor is a great common denominator.

That's true for a very basic reason: humor springs from human nature. And human nature remains the same, whether life is lived in anonymity or on the public stage. It also remains the same through the years, as you'll find in these pages. The quotes here span four generations and nearly a hundred years, from Queen Elizabeth (the Queen Mother) through the young princes, William and Harry.

During that time, the nature of the monarchy has changed. The reserve of the past has given way to a casual breeziness and familiarity. Diana, Princess of Wales, was the first member of the Royal Family to speak directly to the press. Now, there are Royal Family websites and an official website for the British monarchy, as well as a Facebook presence.

The royals' humor encompasses every aspect of their lives, from military service to pursuits such as organic agriculture and sustainable living. They are particularly adept at skewering their own images, and they don't shy away from poking fun at themselves. At other times their words are ironic and self-deprecating, much more introspective than humorous. Their sharpest sarcasm is directed to the media in general and photographers in particular, although a few other targets have also felt the heat—or iciness—of royal voices laden with a withering and sometimes bitter brand of humor.

The chapters in this book range from glimpses inside the walls of the palace to appearances on the world stage, from public image to self-image, and from work to play. To make things a little easier, we refer to each of the royals by a shortened name. Here's a brief look at the members of the Royal Family quoted in this book, and the name used for each:

- Queen Elizabeth, the Queen Mother (the Queen Mum; 1900–2002)

- Her Majesty the Queen, Elizabeth II (Queen Elizabeth; 1926–; daughter of the Queen Mum)

- Princess Margaret (Margaret; 1930–2002; daughter of the Queen Mum)

- Prince Philip, Duke of Edinburgh (Philip; 1921–; married to Queen Elizabeth)

- Prince Charles, Prince of Wales (Charles; 1948–; son of Queen Elizabeth and Philip)

- Princess Anne, the Princess Royal (Anne; 1950–; daughter of Queen Elizabeth and Philip)

- Prince Andrew, Duke of York (Andrew; 1960–; son of Queen Elizabeth and Philip)

- Sarah Ferguson, Duchess of York (Sarah; 1959–; was married to Andrew)

- Prince Edward, Earl of Wessex (Edward; 1964–; son of Queen Elizabeth and Philip)

- Diana, Princess of Wales (Diana; 1961–1997; was married to Charles)

- Prince William (William; 1982–; son of Charles and Diana)

- Catherine Elizabeth "Kate" Middleton (Kate; 1982–; engaged to William in December 2010)

- Prince Harry (Harry; 1984–; son of Charles and Diana)

- Camilla, Duchess of Cornwall (Camilla; 1947–; married to Charles)

As you read through these pages, you're sure to find quotes that will make you laugh. Others will make you cringe, grateful that you weren't the one who said them. Above all, you'll find that behind the mystique of royalty, behind the pomp and pageantry, there are very real, very fallible, and often very funny human beings.

Love
and
Marriage

"It was my duty to marry Bertie and I fell in love with him afterwards."

—The Queen Mum

"Whatever 'in love' means."

—Charles, asked if he was in love, upon announcement of his engagement to Diana

"I'm just coming down to earth."

—Camilla, after announcement of her engagement to Charles

"[Camilla and I are] just a couple of middle-aged people getting wed."

—Charles

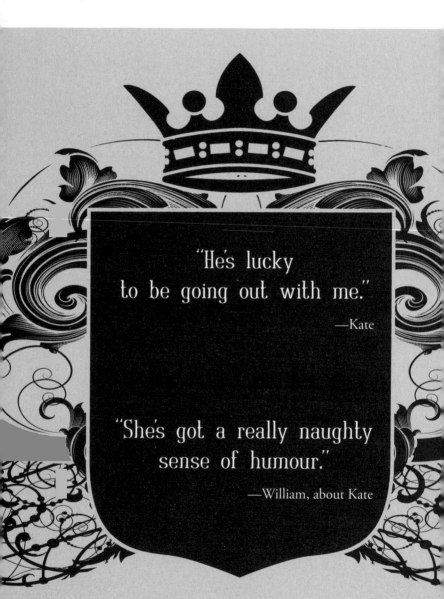

"He's lucky
to be going out with me."

—Kate

"She's got a really naughty
sense of humour."

—William, about Kate

> ## "There wasn't just one, there was about 20."
>
> —William, about the rumor that Kate had a picture of him on her wall at school

> *"He wishes.*
> *No, I had the*
> *Levi's guy on my wall,*
> *not a picture of William, sorry."*
>
> —Kate

> ## "It was me in Levi's obviously."
>
> —William

"Well I actually think I went bright red when I met you and sort of scuttled off, feeling very shy about meeting you."

—Kate

"It's the most brilliant news. I'm just so happy and so are they. It's wicked."

—Camilla, on William and Kate's engagement

"They've been practising for long enough."

—Charles

"I don't remember how many years it's been . . . I also didn't realize it was a race, otherwise I would have been a lot quicker!"

—William, on why it took him so long to propose

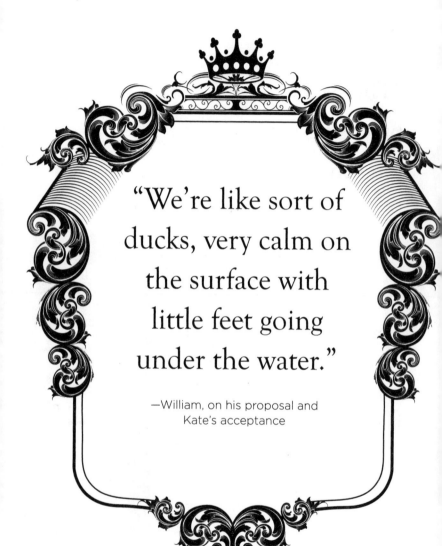

"We're like sort of ducks, very calm on the surface with little feet going under the water."

—William, on his proposal and Kate's acceptance

"It's impossible for anybody else to understand why it has taken me so long [to get married]. But I don't think it had been right before and I don't think Sophie would have said yes. Hopefully the fact that she has said yes means I've got the timing right."

—Edward

"I'd been planning it for a while but as any guy out there will know it takes a certain amount of motivation to get yourself going."

—William, on proposing

"I wanted to give her a chance to see in and to back out if she needed to before it all got too much. I'm trying to learn from lessons done in the past and I just wanted to give her the best chance to settle in and to see what happens on the other side."

—William

"I was torn between asking Kate's dad first and then the realisation that he might actually say 'no' dawned upon me. So I thought if I ask Kate first then he can't really say no."

—William, on whether he'd asked Kate's dad before proposing to her

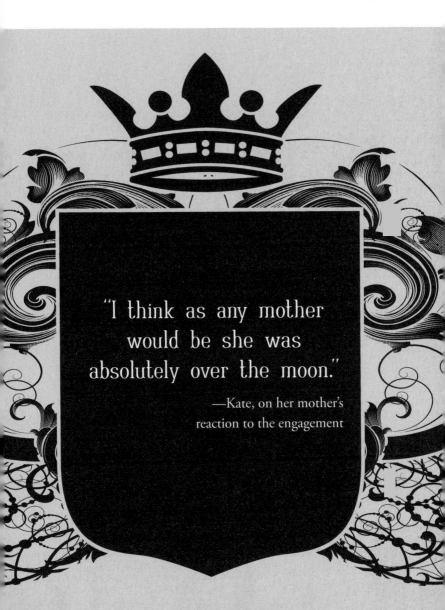

"I think as any mother would be she was absolutely over the moon."

—Kate, on her mother's reaction to the engagement

"Actually we had quite an awkward situation because I knew that William had asked my father but I didn't know if my mother knew."

—Kate

"Let's take one step at a time."

—Edward, when upon his engagement to Sophie was asked about the possibility of starting a family

"I think we'll take it one step at a time. We'll sort of get over the marriage first and then maybe look at the kids."

—William, when asked the same question

"These wretched babies don't come until they are ready."

—The Queen Mum
(also attributed to Queen Elizabeth)

"If men had to have babies, they would only ever have one each."

—Diana

"Being pregnant is a very boring six months. I am not particularly maternal. It's an occupational hazard of being a wife."

—Anne

"I don't like children."

—Anne

"I hate grownups and love children."

—Sarah

"Tolerance is the one essential ingre-dient . . . You can take it from me that the Queen has the quality of tolerance in abundance."

—Philip, when asked about the require-ments for a successful marriage

"*He loves the madness of me.*"

—Sarah

"*I married Her Majesty the Queen's best-looking son.*"

—Sarah

"[I am] not the sort of woman
who is going to meekly trot along
beside her husband."

—Sarah, the day before marrying Andrew

*"People think that at the end
of the day a man is the only
answer. Actually, a fulfilling
job is better for me."*

—Diana

"**Your greatest achievement is to love me.**"

—Charles, to Camilla

"*When a man opens the car door for his wife, it's either a new car or a new wife.*"

—Philip

The
𝕽𝖓𝖔𝖙
𝖀𝖓𝖗𝖆𝖛𝖊𝖑𝖘

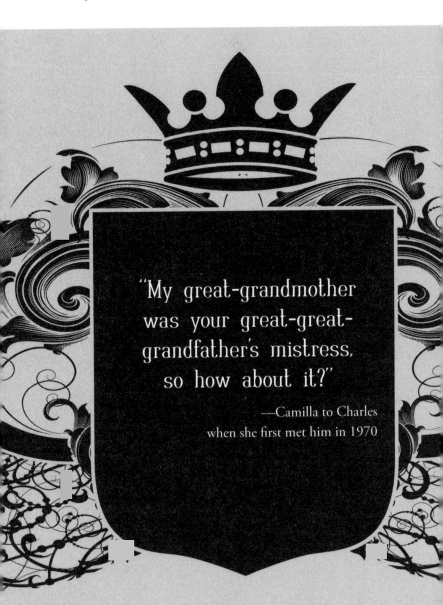

"My great-grandmother was your great-great-grandfather's mistress, so how about it?"

—Camilla to Charles when she first met him in 1970

"There were three of us in this marriage, so it was a bit crowded."

—Diana

"Do you seriously expect me to be the first Prince of Wales in history not to have a mistress?"

—Charles

"You've got everything you ever wanted. You've got all the men in the world falling in love with you and you've got two beautiful children, what more do you want?"

—Camilla to Diana, when confronted about the affair

"I want my husband."

—Diana

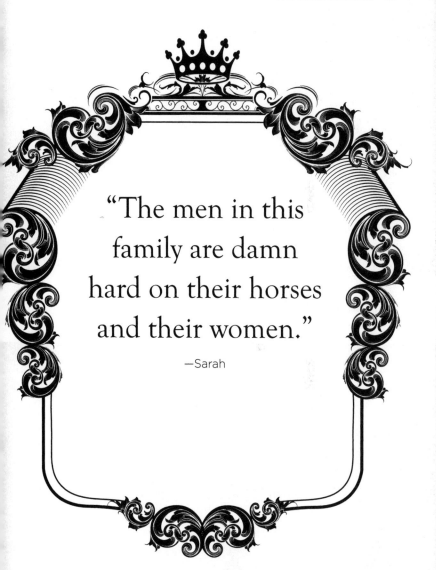

"The men in this family are damn hard on their horses and their women."

—Sarah

"I'm the only woman who has not been beheaded for leaving the Royal Family."

—Sarah

"Any sane person would have left long ago."

—Diana

"She won't go quietly, that's the problem."

—Diana, referring to herself

"Andrew was away at sea 320 days a year. I wanted my man beside me. I was an affair waiting to happen."

—Sarah

"I would like to think that lessons have been learned because my goodness some lessons did need learning."

—Andrew, regarding his failed marriage to Sarah

"I think I was successful in a way, successful at failing."

—Sarah, regarding the marriage

"[I was] so happy and so in love, that I'd forgotten I'd also married 'the firm' and Great Britain and the world. Had I known, I still would have married, but maybe I would have done some things differently."

—Sarah

"*Really, though, he was such a nice person in those days.*"

—Margaret on why she married
Antony Armstrong-Jones

"*He's a fantastic father and friend and you cannot put Andrew and I in a box of any description.*"

—Sarah

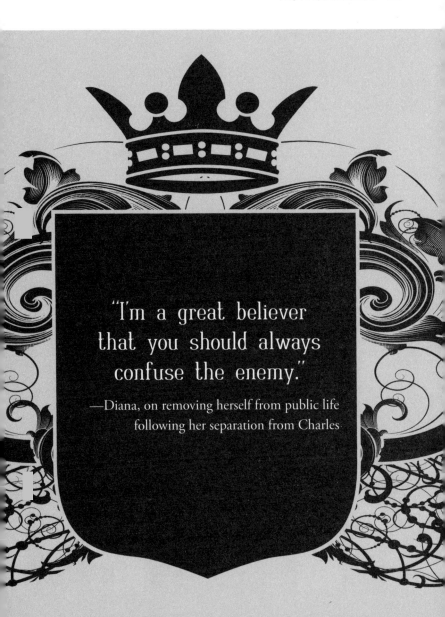

"I'm a great believer that you should always confuse the enemy."

—Diana, on removing herself from public life following her separation from Charles

"We like to say that we are the happiest divorced couple in the world."

—Sarah

"We are the happiest unmarried couple."

—Sarah

*"When you are happy
you can forgive
a great deal."*

—Diana

"Being divorced to,

and not being divorced from."

—Andrew on the secret of a happy divorce

Nearest

and

Dearest

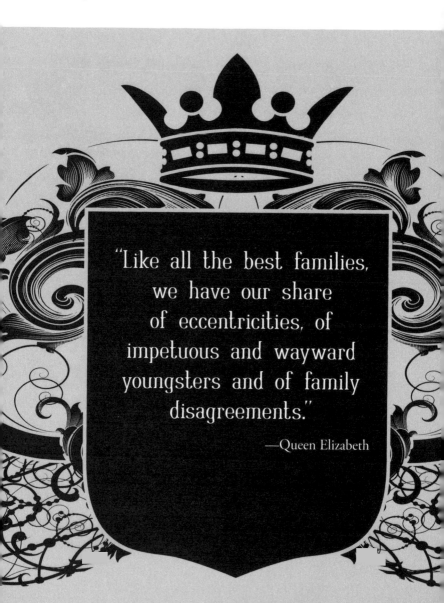

"Like all the best families, we have our share of eccentricities, of impetuous and wayward youngsters and of family disagreements."

—Queen Elizabeth

"Judging by some families I think we are all on pretty good speaking terms after all this time and that's no mean achievement for quite a lot of families."

—Anne

"In our family, we don't have rifts. We have a jolly good row and then it's all over. And I've only twice ever had a row with my sister."

—Margaret

"*Hugs can do great amounts of good—especially for children.*"

—Diana

"*My children are not royal; they just happen to have the Queen for their aunt.*"

—Margaret (also attributed to Queen Elizabeth as "They are not royal. They just happen to have me as their aunt.")

"I suppose, I'll now be known as Charley's Aunt."

—Margaret, referencing the title character of a popular stage play

"I am delighted that my brother has popped the question! It means I get a sister, which I have always wanted."

—Harry

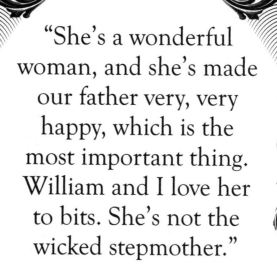

"She's a wonderful woman, and she's made our father very, very happy, which is the most important thing. William and I love her to bits. She's not the wicked stepmother."

—Harry, on Camilla

"The lowest of the low."

—The Queen Mum's opinion of
Wallis Warfield Simpson, for whom Edward VIII,
her brother-in-law, abdicated

"The party is on my birthday, June 21—my 21st on the 21st, which is Midsummer's Day, the longest day of the year and the longest night for a lot of people who are helping to organize it. My father very kindly suggested having a party, although he's probably regretting it now."

—William

"Sarah will talk to me about someone and I don't know who she's talking about, but if she talks to my mother, the two of them will know exactly—and across several generations, too."

—Andrew

"When I think he's wrong I'll tell him he's wrong. Nine times out of ten he puts that in his back pocket and carries on anyway, but in later life who knows?"

—Harry, regarding advice he gives William

"We contact each other the normal way, text messages, phone calls."

—Harry

"Usually means he's left something at home and I have to bring it for him."

—William, regarding phone calls or texts from Harry

"Oh, he's a wild thing,
all right. Yeah."

—William, talking about Harry

"He'd probably sit and play
computer games and drink beer."

—William joking about what Harry
would do if he weren't a Windsor

"He's definitely the more
intelligent one of the two of us."

—Harry, on William

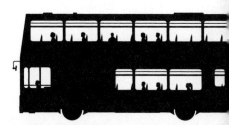

"Not because I look like a wombat. Or maybe I do."

—William, when asked why Diana
nicknamed him "Wombat"

"You know what it was. He was still crawling at six."

—Harry

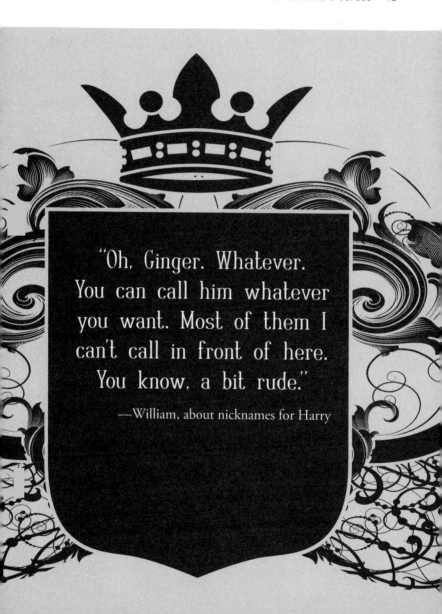

"Oh, Ginger. Whatever.
You can call him whatever
you want. Most of them I
can't call in front of here.
You know, a bit rude."

—William, about nicknames for Harry

"It's not even a contest. Obviously I'd win. Obviously. As the bigger brother you have that psychological power over your brother, you see."

—William, when asked by a young cancer patient whether he or Harry would win at arm-wrestling

"Good to get him out of the house, you know, and get away from us."

—William, regarding the possibility of Harry's military deployment

"Her knowledge of the Army is amazing for a grandmother; I suppose it is slightly her job."

—Harry, about his talks with
Queen Elizabeth about his deployment

"When the question arose whether I, as a member of the Royal Family, should take part in active combat in the Falklands, there was no question in her mind, and it only took her two days to sort the issue."

—Andrew

"Granny, I've got to go. Send my love to the corgis and Grandpa. I've got to go . . . God Save you, yeah, that's great."

—Harry caught on tape making a mock phone call to his grandmother

"I don't want to be liked by someone just because of who I am. You know, I don't want the sycophantic, you know, people hanging around, you know?"

—Harry

"Our friends have to
put up with a lot when it
comes to us."

—Harry

"There's a lot of baggage
that comes with us, trust me,
a lot of baggage."

—William

"The most amusing point is meeting somebody and them going, 'You're so not what I
thought you were.' And to both of us on to,
you know, to our father, to everybody. 'You're
not what I thought you were,' and, 'Well,
what did you think?' 'Oh, I best not say it to
your face,' like this. Well, thanks a lot."

—Harry, on people's impressions of the
Royal Family based on media reports

Life
as a
Royal

"I have as much privacy as a goldfish in a bowl."

—Margaret

"If you live in that goldfish bowl and you are a public figure then to a certain extent you've got to expect somebody to throw a stone and you've got to live with it."

—Andrew

"All the time I feel I must justify my existence."

—Charles

"I knew what my job was; it was to go out and meet the people and love them."

—Diana

"I think people don't quite understand how much it requires to put your head above the parapet. It's no fun having your head shot off all the time."

—Charles

"You stick your head above the parapet and they shoot you down."

—Sarah

"People say to me, Would you like to swap your life with me for twenty-four hours? Your life must be very strange. But of course I have not experienced any other life. It's not strange to me."

—Andrew

"I've had lots of kids come up and ask for my autograph, I've had a grandmother stop and ask me if I know a good place to buy underwear."

—William

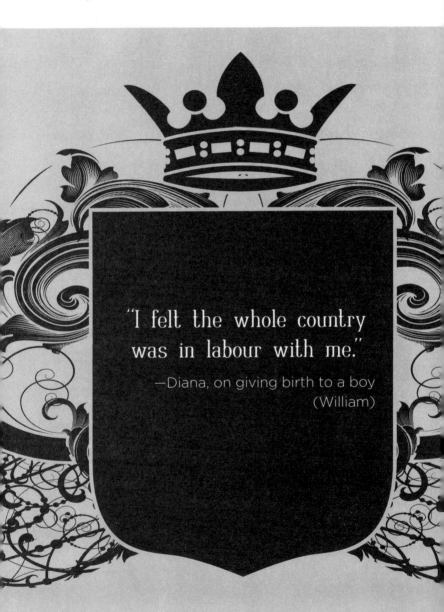

"I felt the whole country was in labour with me."

—Diana, on giving birth to a boy (William)

"When I'm approaching a water jump, with dozens of photographers waiting for me to fall in, and hundreds of spectators wondering what's going to happen next, the horse is just about the only one who doesn't know I am Royal!"

—Anne

"When you're on the public stage, you must smile because nobody wants to see princesses not smiling, nor appreciating what they've got."

—Sarah's advice to her daughters, Eugenie and Beatrice

"I said to them that when they get out of the car, wherever they are in the world, they've got to get out and smile because there's somebody, tenth floor of a building in Oklahoma City or somewhere, they want to see princesses that are smiling, that are from—they're from privilege. They've got great backgrounds. They've got a very lucky life. Now, smile and show the world that it's OK. You can—it is all right. And don't look grumpy and sulky and put your head down. That's a bore."

—Sarah

"The last thing I want to do is cause loads of hype or problems, I just want to go in there and get my asparagus or whatever."

—William, on doing his own shopping

"I hope I'm not a tourist attraction—I'm sure that they come here really because St. Andrews is just amazing, a beautiful place."

—William

"I sometimes wonder if two-thirds of the globe is covered in red carpet."

—Charles

"The man who invented the red carpet needed his head examined."

—Philip

"People come out of curiosity,
if nothing else."

—Charles, on the opportunity
to present his views on crucial issues

"You have to think of the
Royal Family as being like
a brand, yah?"

—Sarah

Public Image
and
Self-Image

"We have an image?
That's news to me."

—William

"It can't be good."

—Harry

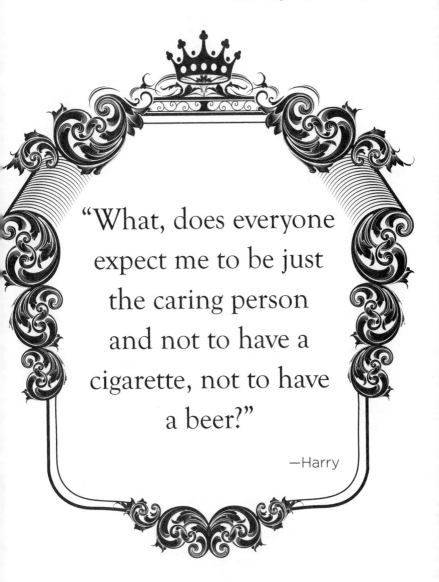

"What, does everyone
expect me to be just
the caring person
and not to have a
cigarette, not to have
a beer?"

—Harry

"When I appear in public people expect me to neigh, grind my teeth, paw the ground and swish my tail—none of which is easy."

—Anne

"It's slightly complicated for people to grasp the idea of a head of state in human form."

—Andrew

"I have to be seen to be believed."

—Queen Elizabeth, regarding going
into crowds of people, chatting,
shaking their hands

"[I'm] not everyone's idea of a fairytale princess."

—Anne

"I'd like to be a queen of people's hearts, in people's hearts, but I don't see myself being Queen of this country. I don't think many people [within the Royal Family] will want me to be Queen."

—Diana

*"I don't go by the rule book . . .
I lead from the heart, not the head."*

—Diana

"I've grown up, everyone's got to grow up.
But there's something inside me that's always
going to be, I'm always going to have that
little sort of—how do you say?—child streak."

—Harry

"I do think I'm a country boy at heart. I love the buzz of towns and going out with friends and sitting with them drinking and whatever—it's fun. But, at the same time, I like space and freedom."

—William

"I'm no angel, but I'm no Bo-Beep either."

—Margaret

"No! Not according to my definition anyway. I'm open to suggestions about what a celebrity actually is but in my definition, no."

—Anne, asked whether she sees herself as a celebrity

"I was very daunted because as far as I was concerned I was a fat, chubby, twenty-year-old, twenty-one-year-old, and I couldn't understand the level of interest."

—Diana, regarding people's interest in her

"If you're born into it I think it's normal to feel as though you don't really want it, if that makes sense."

—Harry, on fame

"I couldn't even begin to tell you the fears [and] the anxieties I had. The only way I could cover it up was to laugh or eat."

—Sarah

"Diana was always the saint, the tall beautiful figure, and I was always this sinner with a rather large bottom."

—Sarah

"It was very difficult when everyone looked at Diana as the most beautiful with the fantastically fabulous figure and then they'd go, 'Oh yes, and her [Sarah].' It was always this feeling when you go to the gym. She's in Lycra and I'm in 'Chariots of Fire' shorts."

—Sarah

"Fat frumpy Fergie."

—Sarah, referring to herself

"With every smell, I smell food. With every sight, I see food. I can almost hear food. I want to spade the whole lot through my mouth at Mach 2. Basta!"

—Sarah

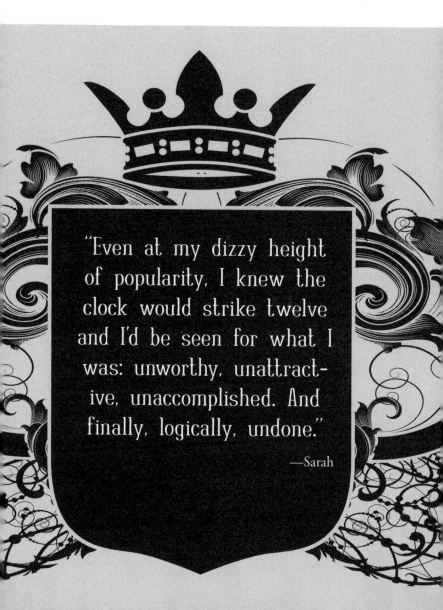

"Even at my dizzy height of popularity, I knew the clock would strike twelve and I'd be seen for what I was: unworthy, unattractive, unaccomplished. And finally, logically, undone."

—Sarah

"I'm always open for people saying I'm wrong because most of the time I am."

—William

"Within our private life and within certain other parts of our life we want to be as normal as possible. . . . It's hard, because to a certain respect we never will be normal."

—Harry, on being part of the Royal Family

"You may be abnormal.
I'm pretty normal."

—William, to Harry

"Deep down
I am pretty normal."

—William

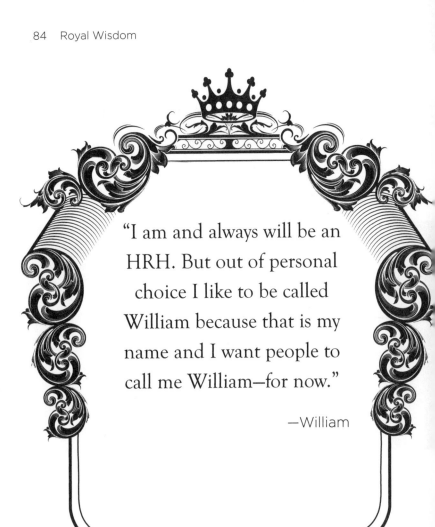

"I am and always will be an HRH. But out of personal choice I like to be called William because that is my name and I want people to call me William—for now."

—William

Military
Service

"There is no way I am going to put myself through Sandhurst and then sit on my arse back home while my boys are out fighting for their country."

—Harry

"[Harry is] going as a guinea pig first to see what happens."

—William, talking about the possibility of going to Sandhurst himself

"The last thing I want to do is be mollycoddled or wrapped up in cotton wool because if I was to join the army, I'd want to go where my men went and I'd want to do what they did."

—William

"It's good fun to be with just a normal bunch of guys, listening to their problems, listening to what they think."

—Harry

"It's very nice to be a sort of normal person for once; I think it's about as normal as I'm going to get."

—Harry, on serving in Afghanistan

"We all lay down on the deck and one of the men had just finished the Rubik's Cube. The Cube was lying in the middle of us and the thought process afterwards was that if we had all been found dead, at least we would have solved the Rubik's Cube."

—Andrew, describing his ship being fired on during the Falklands War

"So, yeah, the Gurkhas think it's hysterical how I'm called the bullet magnet but they've yet to see why."

—Harry

"You could say that,
I'm not too sure,
my history is pretty rubbish."

—Harry, when asked if his level of military
engagement was unusual for the Royal Family

"I do enjoy running
down a ditch full of
mud, firing bullets.
It's the way I am.
I love it."

—Harry

"I haven't managed to dent any of the aircraft, I haven't flown into any trees yet, so, it's going okay."

—William, talking about his flight training

"The simple piece of advice would be 'you should have joined the navy.'"

—Andrew, regarding William serving in the Royal Air Force

Careers

and

Causes

"I could write a really interesting book about finance for women and the first bit of advice I would give is never sign away your intellectual property."

—Sarah

"To win an Oscar . . .
how cool would that be."

—Sarah, talking about her movie project
The Young Victoria

"I don't know how well this would get on,
but I'd probably live in Africa . . . as a
job, it would probably be a safari guide."

—Harry, on what he would do if
he could have any job in the world

"I suppose it is one time when you can really use your name to raise money."

—Harry, about his charity work in Africa

"I could have worse tags than 'Airmiles Andy'—although I don't know what they are."

—Andrew, regarding his travel as a trade representative on behalf of Britain

"I'm not going to be some person in the Royal Family who just finds a lame excuse to go abroad and do all sorts of sunny holidays and whatever."

—Harry

"I could have sat doing very little indeed and I would have been got at just as much by people saying, 'What a useless idiot he is.' So I would rather be criticised for doing things rather than not doing them."

—Charles

"I don't want my grandchildren or yours to come along and say to me, 'Why the hell didn't you do something; you knew what the problem was.'"

—Charles, on his devotion to green energy and sustainable agriculture

"As soon as the word 'holistic' is out of my mouth, I am aware that many people are overcome by a desire to tiptoe to the door and head to the bar to recover."

—Charles

"If you try to kick nature in the teeth and push her too far, she will kick you back."

—Charles

"One of the great difficulties of converting to organic farming turned out to be convincing others that you had not taken complete leave of your senses."

—Charles

"And having the great British public tramping around is hardly organic."

—Anne, referring to equestrian events held at her estate, which is organic grassland

"One common satellite dish means you don't have to have these things stuck all over everything like a rash."

—Charles

"It's funny how some animals go out of fashion."

—Anne, on breeding and raising cattle

"To get the best results, you must talk to your vegetables."

—Charles

"I just come and talk to the plants, really—very important to talk to them, they respond."

—Charles

"I have also put my back into [my gardens], and as a result have probably rendered myself prematurely decrepit in the process."

—Charles

"Only the other day I was inquiring of an entire bed of old-fashioned roses, forced to listen to my ramblings on the meaning of the universe as I sat cross-legged in the lotus position in front of them."

—Charles

"My sense of humor will get me into trouble one day."

—Charles, regarding such things as talking to his plants

Hitting
the
Books

"We've had a good education. Doesn't show, but we have."

—Harry

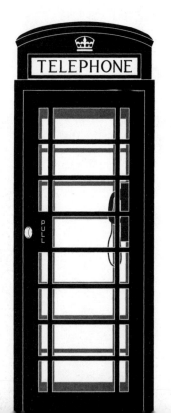

"Harry can paint but I can't. He has our father's talent while I, on the other hand, am about the biggest idiot on a piece of canvas. I did do a couple of drawings at Eton which were put on display. Teachers thought they were examples of modern art, but in fact, I was just trying to paint a house!"

—William

"I just want to go to university and have fun—I want to be an ordinary student. I'm only going to university. It's not like I'm getting married—though that's what it feels like sometimes."

—William

"My father thinks I'm the laziest person on earth."

—William, regarding his time at university

"It has proved a little harder than I thought."

—William, on trying to teach himself Swahili
when he was a student at St. Andrews

"Who's the best pupil? I was always the worst!"

—Harry, joking with ninth-graders
during a U.S. visit

On the
Playing Fields

"I didn't like netball . . . I used to get wolf whistles because of my short skirts."

—Anne

"If it were not for my Archbishop of Canterbury I should be off in my plane to Longchamp [horse-racing course in Paris] every Sunday."

—Queen Elizabeth

"The only active sport I will follow is polo—and most of the work is done by the pony."

—Philip

"It's a bit pathetic."

—Anne, regarding current rules
that would not have allowed her to get back on
her horse after being thrown during the
1976 Montreal Olympic Games

"In my day you were the person
to blame, not the horse."

—Anne, on horsemanship

"Football's a difficult
business and aren't
they prima donnas?"

—Queen Elizabeth to a league chairman

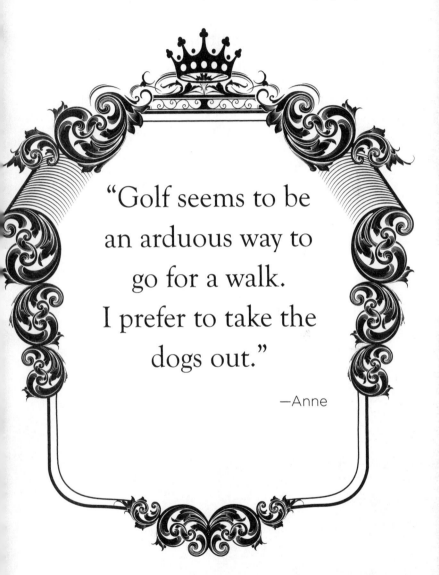

"Golf seems to be an arduous way to go for a walk. I prefer to take the dogs out."

—Anne

"That [being in hospital] was for my Harry Potter scar, as I call it, just here [pointing to his forehead]. I call it that because it glows sometimes and some people notice it— other times they don't notice it at all. I got hit by a golf club when I was playing golf with a friend of mine. Yeah, we were on a putting green and the next thing you know there was a seven-iron and it came out of nowhere and it hit me in the head."

—William

"I'd rather go by bus."

—Charles, regarding trips on the royal yacht

" I'm so glad we've got the yacht with us this time. The last time we came here we had to stay in a guest house. "

—Queen Elizabeth

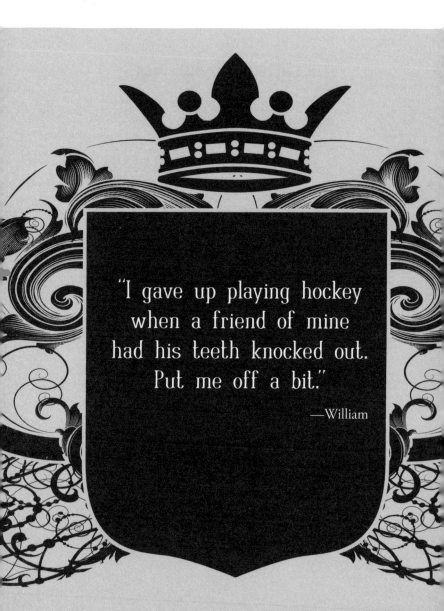

"I gave up playing hockey when a friend of mine had his teeth knocked out. Put me off a bit."

—William

Inside
the
Palace Walls

"The Queen's intelligence network is a hell of a lot better than anyone's in this palace. Bar none. She knows everything. I don't know how she does it. And she sees everything."

—Andrew

"The Queen is the only person who can put on a tiara with one hand, while walking down stairs."

—Margaret

"She is incredibly fit, but we remind staff that she's not just the monarch, but our mother."

—Andrew

"Her friends say she [Queen Elizabeth] is very funny. At a family dinner, she stood to go, and the footman very properly pulled her chair away. At that moment I asked her a question and she sat down again, except there was no chair. Everyone, including the Queen, laughed and laughed."

—Andrew

"If you're not born into royalty, you never really belong there."

—Sarah

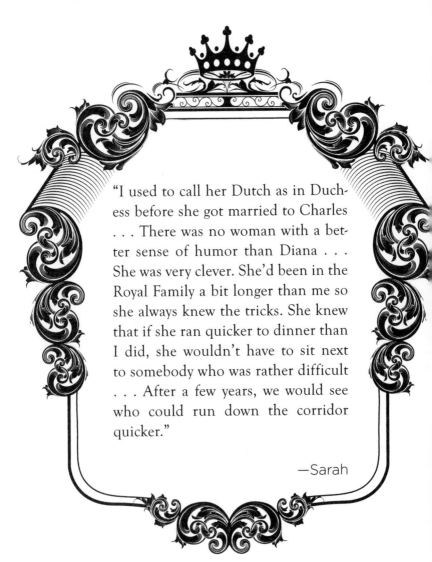

"I used to call her Dutch as in Duchess before she got married to Charles . . . There was no woman with a better sense of humor than Diana . . . She was very clever. She'd been in the Royal Family a bit longer than me so she always knew the tricks. She knew that if she ran quicker to dinner than I did, she wouldn't have to sit next to somebody who was rather difficult . . . After a few years, we would see who could run down the corridor quicker."

—Sarah

"I had to remember my place even though I was a redhead, Irish and a bit temperamental."

—Sarah

"It was dreadful. They tried to put the little redhead in a cage."

—Sarah

"I bounced against walls, the boundaries of life."

—Sarah, on trying to fit into royal life

"I wanted to be perfect, but I should have just stayed this funny old thing."

—Sarah, on doing what she was told at the palace

"Being a princess isn't all it's cracked up to be."

—Diana

"No one sat me down with a piece of paper and said: 'This is what is expected of you.'"

—Diana, on lack of direction from the palace regarding her role as Princess of Wales

"I learned the way a monkey learns—by watching its parents."

—Charles

"You pick it up as you go along. You watch and learn."

—Charles, on the lack of formal training to become king

"I volunteered to go to boarding school. Gets a bit intensive if you're here all the time."

—Anne

Papparazzi
and the
Press

"Bloody people."

—Charles, about the media

"I don't need the press to tell me what to do."

—William

"I had a very bad time with the press—they literally haunted and hunted me. I haven't felt well since day one. I don't think I'm made for the production line."

—Diana, when pregnant with Harry

"You sort of have to ignore a lot of what's said, obviously take it on board, but you have to be yourself really."

—Kate

"I, on the other hand, completely believed every single thing they wrote. I believed I was the worth-less person they were talking about."

—Sarah

"I made the grave mistake once of saying to a child I was thick as a plank, in order to ease the child's nervousness, which it did. But that headline went all round the world, and I rather regret saying it."

—Diana

"It is the media that stamp an image on me that really isn't me."

—Harry

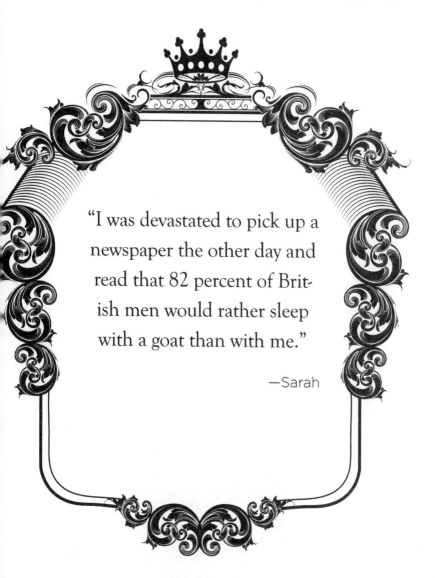

"I was devastated to pick up a newspaper the other day and read that 82 percent of British men would rather sleep with a goat than with me."

—Sarah

"What did I say about drawing the line? That's where it is."

—Anne's reply when asked if she sometimes orders takeout and settles in to watch TV

"They've decided that I'm still a product, after fifteen, sixteen years, that sells well, and they all shout at me, telling me that: 'Oh, come on, Di, look up. If you give us a picture I can get my children to a better school.'"

—Diana

"I have no problem with the freedom of the press . . . but at least have the courage of your pen."

—Sarah, after a columnist wrote a rude comment about her daughter Beatrice and then wouldn't return Sarah's calls about it

"You've got the best view!"

—Harry, while turning away from the press to plant a tree

"Down with the press!"

—Charles

"You have mosquitoes. I have the press."

—Philip, during a tour of the Caribbean

"You are a pest, by the very nature of that camera in your hand."

—Anne

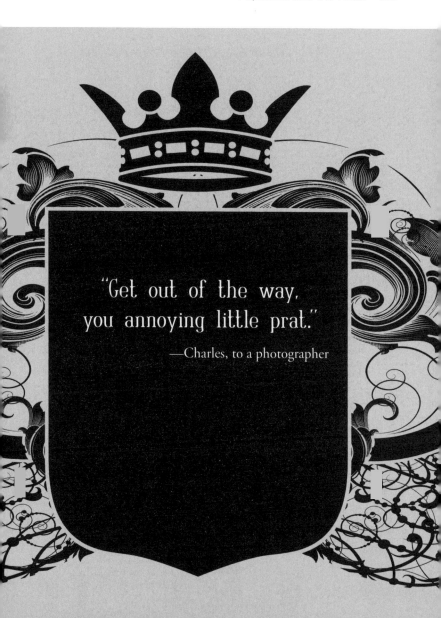

"Get out of the way,
you annoying little prat."

—Charles, to a photographer

*"Have any of you the slightest idea
what I'm doing here?"*

—Charles to the media following
him during an official visit

"There's been a lot of speculation about every single girl I'm with and it actually does quite irritate me after a while, more so because it's a complete pain for the girls."

—William

"Any gentleman that's been past my door, we've instantly been put together in the media and all hell's broken loose, so that's been very tough on the male friends I've had, and obviously from my point of view."

—Diana, on her life after separating from Charles

"I'd probably get myself in a lot of trouble. I'd probably go into the newspaper office, and I'd hide in the background and listen to all the stories they talk about me."

—William, on what he'd do if he could be invisible

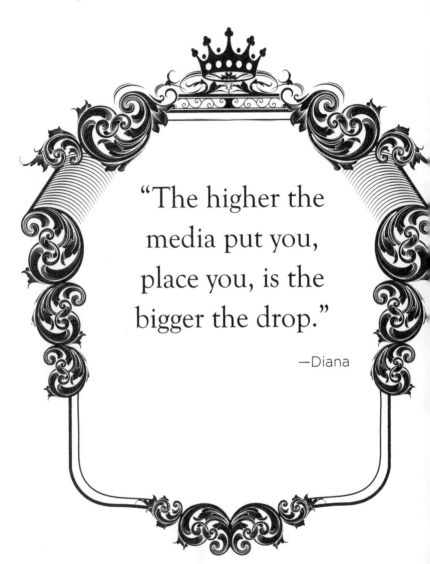

"The higher the media put you, place you, is the bigger the drop."

—Diana

Off the Cuff
and
On the Record

"I'm a dangerous person because I mind about things."

—Charles

"If English is spoken in heaven . . . God undoubtedly employs Cranmer [author of the *Book of Common Prayer*] as his speechwriter. The angels of the lesser ministries probably use the language of the *New English Bible* and the *Alternative Service Book* for internal memos."

—Charles

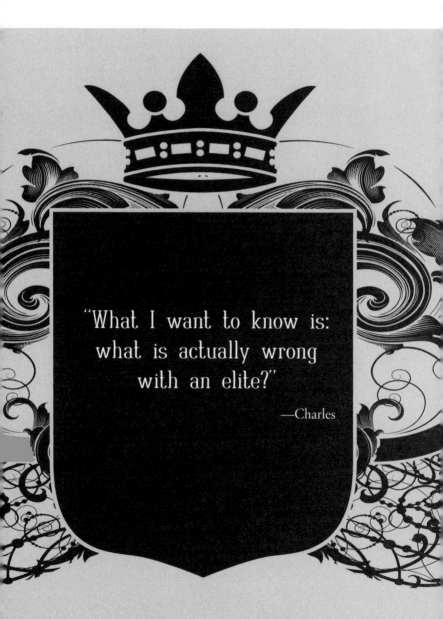

"What I want to know is: what is actually wrong with an elite?"

—Charles

"The whole imposing edifice of modern medicine is like the celebrated tower of Pisa—slightly off balance."

—Charles

"You have to give this much to the Luftwaffe: when it knocked down our buildings it did not replace them with anything more offensive than rubble. We did that."

—Charles

"At the moment it looks as though London seems to be turning into an absurdist picnic table—we already have a giant gherkin, now it looks as if we are going to have an enormous salt cellar."

—Charles, on the design for a new London Bridge Tower

"I mean, you used to put it on the floor, do you remember? And then they put the controls on the bottom so you had to lie on the floor, and then if you wanted to record something the recorder was underneath, so you ended up lying on the floor with a torch in your teeth, a magnifying glass and an instruction book. Either that or you had to employ a grandson of age ten to do it for you."

—Philip, talking about design in general and the TV specifically

"If you gave a seven-year-old a brush and paints he'd produce something like that."

—Philip, after looking at some of the paintings in Sudan's ethnic museum

"Ghastly."

—Philip, regarding Beijing, China

"The best that can be said about genetically engineered crops is that they will now be monitored to see how much damage they cause."

—Charles

"We live in an age of rights. It seems to me that it is about time our Creator had some rights, too."

—Charles, talking about genetically modified organisms

"The biggest waste of water in the country is when you spend half a pint and flush two gallons."

—Philip

"It seems to me that it's the best way of wasting money that I know of. I don't think investments on the moon pay a very high dividend."

—Philip, on the U.S. *Apollo* space program

"If you travel as much as we do, you appreciate how much more comfortable aircraft have become. Unless you travel in something called economy class, which sounds ghastly."

—Philip

"I don't think a prostitute is more moral than a wife, but they are doing the same thing."

—Philip, on whether those who sell meat from slaughtered animals are somehow more moral than those who hunt and kill game

"The difficult thing is asking them to pick it up without getting stabbed."

—Charles, referring to antisocial behavior among youths, when asked if he would pick up litter dropped by someone else

"If it has got four legs and is not a chair, if it has two wings and it flies but is not an aeroplane, and if it swims and is not a submarine, the Cantonese will eat it."

—Philip, at a World Wildlife Fund conference

"British women can't cook. They are very good at decorating food and making it attractive. But they have an inability to cook."

—Philip

"The best thing to do with a degree is to forget it."

—Philip, speaking at the University of Salford

"Everybody was saying we must have more leisure. Now they are complaining they are unemployed."

—Philip

"Dontopedalogy is the science of opening your mouth and putting your foot in it, a science which I have practiced for a good many years."

—Philip, speaking to the General Dental Council

"I can only assume that it is largely due to the accumulation of toasts to my health over the years that I am still enjoying a fairly satisfactory state of health and have reached such an unexpectedly great age."

—Philip

"The British Constitution has always been puzzling and always will be."

—Queen Elizabeth

"It is easy enough to define what the Commonwealth is not. Indeed this is quite a popular pastime."

—Queen Elizabeth

"Something as curious as the monarchy won't survive unless you take account of people's attitudes. After all, if people don't want it, they won't have it."

—Charles

"We lost the American colonies because we lacked the statesmanship to know the right time and the manner of yielding what is impossible to keep."

—Queen Elizabeth

Quick Takes

"Golly, I could do with £100,000, couldn't you? I had such an awful afternoon with my bank manager scolding me about my overdraft."

—The Queen Mum

"No, not your typical Christmas but Christmas is overrated anyway."

—Harry, while serving in Afghanistan

"What do you gargle with—pebbles?"

—Philip, to singer Tom Jones

"If you'd spent most of your life on a warship you would not know about taste."

—The Queen Mum, regarding Andrew's home (Sunninghill)

"Her behavior was a bit odd. I don't see her because I do not see much point."

—Philip, about Sarah

"It's a bit draughty."

—William, on wearing a kilt

"I am a closet American."

—Sarah

"I really need a gin and tonic."

—Camilla, after tea and conversation with William at their first meeting (1998)

"There are now more TVs in British households than there are people—which is a bit of a worry."

—Charles

"Travel by helicopter? I think the chopper has changed my life—rather as it did Anne Boleyn's."

—The Queen Mum

"1992 is not a year on which I shall look back with undiluted pleasure."

—Queen Elizabeth

"Hernia today, gone tomorrow."

—Charles, after an operation

"I have not got a bean to my name. I'm a tax-payer, a British taxpayer and I left the Royal Family for freedom and in freedom it means I am bereft. I'm hope-less."

—Sarah

"We don't come here for our health. We can think of other ways of enjoying ourselves."

—Philip, during a trip to Canada

"It's something that we bomb around the fields on—it's a way of shaking the cobwebs out."

—Harry, on biking

"We had this rather lugubrious man in a suit and he read a poem . . . I think it was called 'The Desert' . . . At first the girls got the giggles, then I did, then even the King."

—The Queen Mum, speaking about T. S. Eliot reading "The Waste Land"

"I'm the heir apparent to the heir presumptive."

—Margaret

"I've got no leg and an arm on one side, and no arm and a leg on the other."

—Camilla, joking about having a broken leg and a strained shoulder tendon at the same time

"Father told me that if I ever met a lady in a dress like yours, I must look her straight in the eyes."

—Charles

"Free your mind and your bottom will follow."

—Sarah

"Darling, darling come and see what I have got for you."

—Charles, when giving Camilla a necklace designed to protect the wearer from vampire bites

"Oh, it's quite all right, we curse quite a lot around here."

—Camilla to Sharon Osbourne, after a profanity-laced compliment

"Was that 'dutiful' or 'beautiful'?"

—Harry teasing William about being considered dutiful

"I certainly had my bumps in life in front of the world."

—Sarah

"I liked the old Labour Party. The best thing is a good old Tory government with a strong Labour opposition."

—The Queen Mum

"I hope I'm not going to spill it. Who is going to drink this afterwards? Any takers?"

—Camilla, pulling a pint on the set of the TV program *Coronation Street*

"That, for me, is what British food is really about; a chicken, that has lived a natural life, pecking and scratching about in the yard, roasted until golden brown."

—Camilla

"I don't even know how to use a parking meter, let alone a phone box."

—Diana

"I never liked the idea of the Royal Family film. I always thought it was a rotten idea."

—Anne, about a film that followed the Royal Family for a year

"This sculpture is, um, interesting."

—Andrew, asked to remark at the unveiling of a
modern sculpture

"That's called a microphone. It's a big sausage that picks up everything you say—and you're starting early."

—Charles, to William at his first
press conference, at the age of two

"Only the mad girls chase me, I think."

—William

"I don't think any man would keep up. It would have to be someone who puts up with the press as well and with a strong redhead."

—Sarah

"I have always had a dread of becoming a passenger in life."

—Margaret

"Everyone is really well looked-after here by the Gurkhas, the food is fantastic—goat curries, chicken curries—probably shouldn't say goat curries, but yeah, it's really good fun and, yeah, we're really well looked after."

—Harry

"Where's your sense of humor tonight?"

—Sarah, trying to make light of being caught on film offering to sell business access to Andrew to a man who was a stranger to her

"By far the best dressing up outfit I ever had was a wonderful pair of clown dungarees, which my Granny made."

—Kate

"I had a heavy day."

—Sarah, referring to the sting

"Actually, when I was going to talk to you about my books, I suddenly realised that maybe I should take a leaf out of my own books . . . one of my books is *Ashley Learns About Strangers*."

—Sarah, speaking at a book fair after the scandal broke

"Define useful."

—William, when asked by an interviewer whether
he does anything useful around the house

"I get quite lazy about cooking because when I come back from work it is the last thing I want to do, really is spend loads of time cooking. When I was trying to impress Kate I was trying to cook these amazing fancy dinners and what would happen was I would burn something, something would overspill, something would catch on fire and she would be sitting in the background just trying to help, and basically taking control of the whole situation, so I was quite glad she was there at the time."

—William

"To be honest they were used to it, watching things catching fire, they found it very amusing."

—William, to the same interviewer, on the other flatmates' reaction to the cooking mishaps

"I would not like to feel I had lived all these years without having anything to show for it."

—The Queen Mum, regarding retouching a photo to remove her wrinkles

"We have learned that real life is too extreme for fiction."

—Sarah

"I don't know, I'm a little bit more ginger [red-haired] in there than I am in real life, I think, I don't know, and William got given more hair so, apart from that, it is what it is, but no it's nice, it could have been worse."

—Harry, regarding the first double portrait of him and William

"It was a poor choice of costume."

—Harry, about dressing as a Nazi for a costume party

"There's new paintwork, are you sure you trust me with it?"

—Camilla, upon taking the helm of a boat

"I think that I will take two small bottles of Dubonnet and gin with me this morning, in case it is needed."

—The Queen Mum, in a note written to her favorite page before leaving for an outdoor lunch

"I never see any home cooking—
all I get is fancy stuff."

—Philip

"I am very glad you have heard of it."

—Charles, responding to media questions about
his impending marriage to Camilla

*"I don't want to sound desperate,
but I'd like someone to come and
join me on Planet Sarah."*

—Sarah, regarding finding another man

"Where did you get the hat?"

—Philip to Queen Elizabeth after her coronation

Spine
and
Spirit

"Not bloody likely."

—Anne, diving out the door after an armed gun-man ambushed her car and demanded £2 million ($4.6 million) during a kidnap attempt in 1974

"[There's a] first time for everything."

—Camilla, laughing off the attack on her and Charles during the student protests

"Look around at other members of my family who are considerably older than me, and tell me whether they've set an example that makes you think I might. Unlikely."

—Anne's withering response to an interviewer asking whether, having turned sixty, she might slow down

"It's just another birthday."

—Anne

"I am in the kindergarten of middle age!"

—Sarah

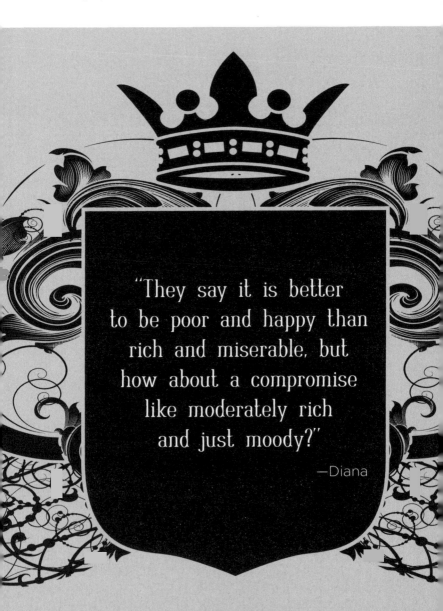

"They say it is better
to be poor and happy than
rich and miserable, but
how about a compromise
like moderately rich
and just moody?"

—Diana

"Oh, dear, I hope it wasn't anyone important."

—Queen Elizabeth, to Parliament member Clare Short when Short's cell phone rang during a private Privy Council meeting with the Queen

"We are just little atoms, circling around and doing our own thing."

—Sarah

"I like to be a free spirit. Some don't like that, but that's the way I am."

—Diana

"How reassuring."

—Queen Elizabeth, when told during a walking tour of Scotland that she looks like the Queen

"Life is just a journey."

—Diana

"Actually, Captain, I think it's me they've come to see."

—Queen Elizabeth, to an escort commander blocking the crowd's view of the State Carriage during an official visit

"I've learned how to play the chic game of chess of life."

—Sarah

Can I

Rephrase

That?

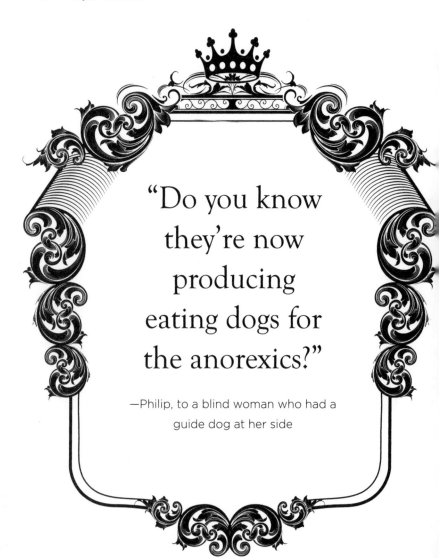

"Do you know they're now producing eating dogs for the anorexics?"

—Philip, to a blind woman who had a guide dog at her side

"Are you Indian or Pakistani? I can never tell the difference between you chaps."

—Philip, at a Washington Embassy reception for Commonwealth members

"Do you still throw spears at each other?"

—Philip, speaking to Australian Aborigines

"Deaf? If you are near there, no wonder you are deaf."

—Philip, to a group of deaf children gathered near a Jamaican steel drum band

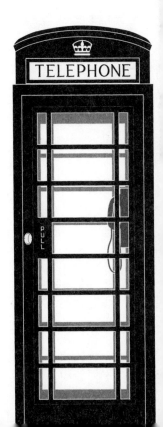

"How do you keep the natives off the booze long enough to pass the test?"

—Philip, to a Scottish driving instructor

"If you stay here much longer you'll all be slitty-eyed."

—Philip, speaking to British students in China

"Since the charity [Age Concern] was established in 1949 thousands of elderly people in Wiltshire have benefited from its many services ranging from home support to luncheon and technology clubs and toenail cutting which I am very interested by."

—Camilla

"It looks as if it was put in by an Indian."

—Philip, as he pointed at a fuse box

"Bloody silly fool!"

—Philip, when he wasn't recognized by a parking attendant at Cambridge University

"Aren't most of you descended from pirates?"

—Philip, visiting the Cayman Islands

"You managed not to get eaten, then."

—Philip, speaking to a student who had been traveling in Papua New Guinea

"Aren't there any male supervisors? This is a nanny city."

—Philip, in San Francisco, upon meeting five city officials, all of them female

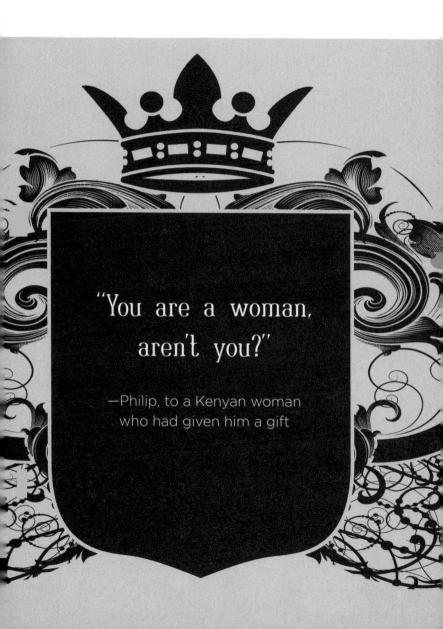

"You are a woman, aren't you?"

—Philip, to a Kenyan woman
who had given him a gift

"You can't have been here that long—you haven't got a pot belly."

—Philip, speaking to a Briton in Budapest

"Ah good, there's so many over there you feel they breed them just to put in orphanages."

—Philip, asking a student whether he'd helped the Romanian orphans during the time he'd worked in that country

"Well, you'll never fly in it, you're too fat to be an astronaut."

—Philip, to a thirteen-year-old who said he'd like to fly a spacecraft Philip was inspecting

"There's a lot of your family in tonight."

—Philip, to a man who had the common Indian surname "Patel," at a reception for 400 British Indian businessmen

"Are you all one family?"

—Philip, to a black dance troupe

"English students don't spend much time on their studies. They're more interested in partying and having fun."

—Camilla, comparing them to Pakistani students

"Oh, what, a strip club?"

—Philip, speaking to a female navy cadet who had told him that she'd worked in a club

"The problem with London is the tourists. They cause the congestion. If we could just stop tourism, we could stop the congestion."

—Philip

"If a cricketer, for example, suddenly decided to go into a school and batter a lot of people to death with a cricket bat, which he could do very easily, I mean, are you going to ban cricket bats?"

—Philip talking about calls for a ban on firearms after sixteen schoolchildren and their teacher were killed

"Can't understand a word they say. They slur all their words."

—Philip, referring to French Canadians

"I must confess that I am tempted to ask for reincarnation as a particularly deadly virus."

—Philip, in his foreword to the book *If I Were an Animal*

Sources

http://abcnews.go.com/GMA/Media/fergie-duchess-york-scandal-queen-crisis-talks-prince/
    story?id=10731971&page=2

http://au.lifestyle.yahoo.com/who/latest-news/article/-/8335456/prince-charles-reacts-to-royal-
    wedding-with-humour

http://blog.gaiam.com/quotes/uuthors/sarah-ferguson

http://blog.lib.umn.edu/robe0419/coffee/2005_10.html

http://books.google.com/books?id=_fkiC8lg6jQC&pg=PA19&lpg=PA19&dq=if+english+is+
    spoken+in+heaven&source=bl&ots=XYcaVXdzYw&sig=1ZG1rom250FOFPFalG_GxFu-
    qPw&hl=en&ei=4Z0eTb2wHMOB8gaZi735DQ&sa=X&oi=book_result&ct=result&res
    num=5&ved=0CC4Q6AEwBA#v=onepage&q=if%20english%20is%20spoken%20in%20
    heaven&f=false

http://celebrity.uk.msn.com/photos/photos.aspx?cp-documentid=155299881&page=12

http://duchess-of-cornwall-news.newslib.com/story/4201-3042227

http://duchess-of-cornwall-news.newslib.com/story/4201-3042259

http://entertainment.timesonline.co.uk/tol/arts_and_entertainment/tv_and_radio/article7015632
    .ece

http://festivalinsider.ca/2009/09/20/sarah-ferguson-the-young-victoria-tiff-toronto

http://findarticles.com/p/news-articles/daily-mail-london-england-the/mi_8002/is_2001_June_8/
    philip-isms/ai_n36347851

http://forums.canadiancontent.net/news/90025-mark-his-50th-birthday-prince.html

http://listverse.com/2007/09/11/top-15-quotes-of-prince-philip

http://news.bbc.co.uk/2/hi/7269743.stm

http://news.bbc.co.uk/2/hi/uk_news/1848553.stm

http://news.bbc.co.uk/2/hi/uk_news/249529.stm

http://news.bbc.co.uk/2/hi/uk_news/416992.stm

http://news.bbc.co.uk/2/hi/uk_news/7269936.stm

http://news.bbc.co.uk/2/hi/uk_news/8699211.stm

http://news.scotsman.com/dukeofedinburgh/Duke-under-fire-for-Romanian.2790689.jp

http://news.sky.com/skynews/Home/UK-News/Duke-Of-Yorks-Prince-Andrew-Speaks-To-Sky-
    News-To-Mark-His-50th-Birthday/Article/201002215548548

http://ngm.nationalgeographic.com/2006/05/duchy-cornwall/mitchell-text/3

http://nymag.com/news/intelligencer/encounter/62658

http://showbizandstyle.inquirer.net/entertainment/entertainment/view/20091001-227899/A-chat-
    with-Duchess-Fergie

http://thinkexist.com/quotes/elizabeth,_the_queen_mother

http://thinkexist.com/quotes/elizabeth_ii

http://thinkexist.com/quotes/kate_middleton

http://thinkexist.com/quotes/prince_andrew

http://thinkexist.com/quotes/prince_harry

http://thinkexist.com/quotes/prince_philip,_duke_of_edinburgh

http://thinkexist.com/quotes/prince_william

http://thinkexist.com/quotes/princess_margaret

http://thinkexist.com/quotes/sarah_ferguson/2.html

http://transcripts.cnn.com/TRANSCRIPTS/0310/21/lkl.00.html

www.allgreatquotes.com/camilla_parker_bowles_quotes.shtml

www.allgreatquotes.com/prince_charles_quotes.shtml

www.allgreatquotes.com/prince_harry_quotes.shtml

www.allgreatquotes.com/princess_diana_quotes2.shtml

www.allgreatquotes.com/queen_elizabethii_quotes.shtml

www.amusingquotes.com/h/c/Prince_Charles_1.htm

www.angelfire.com/on/kittywinky/home.html

www.answers.com/topic/charles-prince-of-wales

www.bbc.co.uk/dna/h2g2/A4158371

www.bbc.co.uk/politics97/diana/panorama.html

www.bbc.co.uk/pressoffice/pressreleases/stories/2002/04_april/29/princessanne_interview.shtml

www.bookrags.com/quotes/Elizabeth_II_of_the_United_Kingdom

www.brainyquote.com/quotes/authors/e/elizabeth_ii.html

www.brainyquote.com/quotes/authors/k/kate_middleton.html

www.brainyquote.com/quotes/authors/p/prince_andrew.html

www.brainyquote.com/quotes/authors/p/prince_charles.html

www.brainyquote.com/quotes/authors/p/prince_wllliam.html

www.brainyquote.com/quotes/authors/p/princess_diana_2.html

www.brainyquote.com/quotes/authors/p/princess_margaret.html

www.brainyquote.com/quotes/authors/s/sarah_ferguson.html

www.bt.com.bn/classification/life/features/2007/04/02/palace_was_a_bleak_house_says_sarah

www.cbc.ca/world/story/2009/02/06/f-prince-philip.html

www.cbsnews.com/stories/2005/09/16/listening_post/main853201.shtml

www.countrylife.co.uk/property/guidesrenovations/article/313347/Princess-Royal-interview.html

www.dailymail.co.uk/femail/article-1083787/As-Prince-Charles-turns-60-exclusive-insight-man-
    king-lives-long-enough.html

www.dailymail.co.uk/femail/article-1302639/The-best-king-Why-Princess-Anne-man-brothers-
    lot-interesting-too.html

www.dailymail.co.uk/news/article-1032397/Queen-Mothers-note-requesting-Dubonnet-gin-
    fetches-16-000.html

www.dailymail.co.uk/news/article-112126/My-loving-mother-Princess-Anne.html#ixzz18Dvsdz8u

www.dailymail.co.uk/news/article-1163000/Who-gave-Prince-William-Harry-Potter-scar-Royal-
    reveals-friend-hit-golf-club.html

www.dailymail.co.uk/news/article-1250709/EXCLUSIVE-Prince-Andrew-talks-frankly-living-
    Fergie-denies-freeloader--launches-scathing-attack-greed-bankers-politicians.html

www.dailymail.co.uk/news/article-1333035/Ive-got-to-work-Another-classic-gaffe-Prince-Philip-
    refuses-shake-hands-royal-visit.html

www.dailymail.co.uk/news/worldnews/article-1281708/Sarah-Ferguson-jokes-U-S-book-fair-I-
    learn-beware-strangers.html

www.dailymail.co.uk/tvshowbiz/article-1079201/Beatrice-Eugenie-dont-want-marry-reveals-Sarah-Ferguson.html

www.dailymail.co.uk/tvshowbiz/article-1197263/Friendlier-Prince-Andrew-ex-wife-Sarah-Ferguson-meet-dinner-date.html#ixzz19djkY7wq

www.debt1.co.uk/news/duchess-of-york-may-require-debt-management-19435493

www.designcouncil.org.uk/Files/Transcripts/Video-transcripts/Prince-Philip-and-Kevin-McCloud

www.exposay.com/v/32066/duchess-cornwall-camilla-given-necklace-protection-against

www.express.co.uk/posts/view/2273

www.famousquotesandauthors.com/authors/princess_anne_quotes.html

www.foxnewsinsider.com/2010/11/16/quick-quote-prince-harry-on-williams-engagement

www.goodreads.com/author/quotes/1179014.Prince_Charles

www.greatpersonalities.com/prince-harry

www.great-quotes.com/quote/1908150

www.guardian.co.uk/lifeandstyle/2009/jun/07/did-i-say-that-prince-charles

www.guardian.co.uk/uk/2002/mar/31/queenmother.monarchy2

www.hellomagazine.com/royalty/200909071969/sarah-ferguson/fergie-young-victoria/oscar/1

www.hellomagazine.com/royalty/201004223349/camilla/leg-wheelchair/shoulder/1

www.highbeam.com/doc/1G1-60878996.html

www.houmatoday.com/article/20101123/ENTERTAINMENT/101119207?p=2&tc=pg

www.huffingtonpost.com/.../sarah-ferguson-duchess-of_b_394824.html

www.huffingtonpost.com/social/bubbuh/prince-william-shadow-kin_n_390010_36232068.html

www.imdb.com/title/tt0251380/

www.independent.co.uk/news/people/profiles/prince-philip-royal-flash-889303.html

www.independent.co.uk/news/people/profiles/sarah-duchess-of-york-red-alert-830016.html

www.independent.co.uk/news/uk/home-news/princess-margaret-in-quotes-660223.html

www.iwise.com/Duke_of_Edinburgh_Philip

www.mirror.co.uk/news/top-10s/2009/12/14/gift-of-the-gaffe-prince-philip-s-top-ten-embarrassing-moments-115875-21896895

www.mirror.co.uk/news/top-stories/2009/12/20/are-you-all-one-family-philip-asks-
   diversity-115875-21910150

www.mirror.co.uk/news/top-stories/2010/03/12/philip-and-cadet-24-in-strip-
   tease-115875-22105123

www.mirror.co.uk/news/top-stories/2010/08/14/the-real-anne-115875-22486553

www.msnbc.msn.com/id/19190534/ns/dateline_nbc-a_conversation_with_william_and_harry

www.nationmultimedia.com/home/Prince-Charles-No-training-to-become-king-30142780.html

www.nytimes.com/2007/04/25/dining/25prin.html?_r=2&scp=5&sq=Prince%20Charles&st=cse

www.parade.com/celebrity/2009/12/sarah-ferguson.html

www.parenthood.com/printarticle.php?Article_ID=7762

www.people.com/people/article/0,,1105497,00.html

www.people.com/people/article/0,,20387587,00.html

www.people.com/people/gallery/0,,20042722_20061387,00.html

www.people.com/people/gallery/0,,20282979_20630458,00.html

www.popeater.com/2010/11/20/quips-quotes-prince-william-kate-middleton

www.princeofwales.gov.uk/newsandgallery/news/prince_harry_gives_an_interview_to_mark_
   his_21st_birthday_pa_1743836799.html

www.princeofwales.gov.uk/newsandgallery/news/prince_william_is_interviewed_for_his_21st_
   birthday_part_2_501917688.html

www.quoteid.com/Prince_Philip,_Duke_of_Edinburgh.html

www.quotesandpoem.com/quotes/listquotes/author/kate-middleton

www.quotesmachine.com/sarah-ferguson-quotes

www.quotesstar.com/people/occupations/prince-philip-duke-of-edinburgh-quotes.html

www.rdmag.com/News/FeedsAP/2009/10/life-sciences-history-not-activism-seems-to-drive-
   prince-charl

www.reuters.com/article/idUSTRE64M0Y220100524?pageNumber=2

www.royal.gov.uk/Home.aspx

www.royaltyinthenews.com/tag/duchess-of-cornwall

www.saidwhat.co.uk/quotes/famous/prince_edward

www.saidwhat.co.uk/quotes/famous/prince_harry/its_something_that_we_bomb_around_22914

www.saidwhat.co.uk/quotes/famous/queen_elizabeth_ii

www.saidwhat.co.uk/quotes/favourite/prince_charles

www.saidwhat.co.uk/quotes/favourite/princess_margaret

www.sheknows.com/entertainment/articles/812655/duchess-sarah-ferguson-a-royal-interview

www.slipups.com/items/16380.html

www.telegraph.co.uk/news/newstopics/theroyalfamily/4864811/Sarah-Duchess-of-York-exclusive-The-only-thing-I-ever-succeeded-at-was-failure.html

www.telegraph.co.uk/news/newstopics/theroyalfamily/7228468/Duke-of-York-Falklands-turned-me-into-a-man.html

www.telegraph.co.uk/news/newstopics/theroyalfamily/7939555/In-praise-of-the-Princess-Royal-Anne-at-60.html

www.telegraph.co.uk/news/newstopics/theroyalfamily/8193133/Royal-car-attack-Duchess-of-Cornwall-laughs-off-student-protest-fees-scare.html

www.telegraph.co.uk/news/uknews/1393020/Philip-tells-blind-woman-Theyve-got-eating-dogs-for-anorexics.html

www.telegraph.co.uk/news/uknews/1580245/Prince-Harry-returns-Queen-speaks-of-pride.html

www.telegraph.co.uk/news/uknews/royal-wedding/8138904/Royal-Wedding-Prince-William-and-Kate-Middleton-interview-in-full.html

www.thefreelibrary.com/AND+FINALLY..+Her+world+Her+words%3B+ELIZABETH+BOWES+LYON+1900+-+2002.-a084295213

www.theroyalforums.com/forums/f34/prince-william-interview-november-2004-a-4131.html

www.time.com/time/magazine/article/0,9171,1181623-2,00.html

www.time.com/time/specials/2007/article/0,28804,1663317_1663319_1669898,00.html

www.time.com/time/world/article/0,8599,1871523,00.html

www.timesonline.co.uk/tol/news/uk/article3455716.ece

www.timesonline.co.uk/tol/news/uk/article5490538.ece

www.upi.com/topic/Kate_Middleton/quotes

www.usatoday.com/life/2003-06-12-william-cover_x.htm

www.vanityfair.com/online/daily/2010/10/exclusive-prince-charles-discusses-the-environment-the-monarchy-his-sons-camilla-his-book-and-islam.html

www.wiltshiretimes.co.uk/news/inyourtown/wiltshire/8379741.Camilla_steers_clear_of_trouble_on_canal_visit_to_Wiltshire

www.woopidoo.com/business_quotes/authors/prince-charles/index.htm